AYE-AYE

By Colleen Sexton

Consultant: Darin Collins, DVM
Director, Animal Health Programs, Woodland Park Zoo

BEARPORT
PUBLISHING

Minneapolis, Minnesota

Credits

cover, © javarman/Shutterstock; 3, © javarman/Shutterstock; 4, © Cagan Hakki Sekercioglu/ Getty Images; 6, © Michael0706/Shutterstock; 7, © Anna Veselova/Shutterstock; 9, © Gallo Images/Getty Images; 10, © Chris Hellier/Alamy Stock Photo; 11, © Danita Delimont/Alamy Stock Photo; 13, © nokwant/Shutterstock; 13, © Suzi Eszterhas/Minden Pictures; 14, © Maks Narodenko/ Shutterstock; 14, © Picsfive/Shutterstock; 15, © Anna Veselova/Shutterstock; 16, © Dudarev Mikhail/Shutterstock; 17, © A & J Visage/Alamy Stock Photo; 19, © imageBROKER/Alamy Stock Photo; 20, © Rob Cousins/Alamy Stock Photo; 23, © Dennis Van De Water/Dreamstime

President: Jen Jenson
Director of Product Development: Spencer Brinker
Editor: Allison Juda
Designer: Micah Edel

Library of Congress Cataloging-in-Publication Data

Names: Sexton, Colleen A., 1967- author.
Title: Aye-aye / Colleen Sexton.
Description: Minneapolis, Minnesota : Bearport Publishing Company, [2021] |
   Series: Library of awesome animals | Includes bibliographical references and index.
Identifiers: LCCN 2020008628 (print) | LCCN 2020008629 (ebook) |
   ISBN 9781647471408 (library binding) | ISBN 9781647471514 (paperback) |
   ISBN 9781647471620 (ebook)
Subjects: LCSH: Aye-aye—Juvenile literature.
Classification: LCC QL737.P935 S49 2021 (print) | LCC QL737.P935 (ebook)
   | DDC 599.8/3—dc23
LC record available at https://lccn.loc.gov/2020008628
LC ebook record available at https://lccn.loc.gov/2020008629

For more information, write to Bearport Publishing, 5357 Penn Avenue South, Minneapolis, MN 55419. Printed in the United States of America.

Contents

AWESOME
Aye-Ayes!

TWITCH! Huge ears perk up above big, staring eyes. **WHOOSH!** A bushy tail swishes by. This crazy creature is an aye-aye. Aye-ayes are awesome!

AN AYE-AYE'S TAIL IS LONGER THAN ITS BODY.

What Is It?

The aye-aye was a mystery when it was first discovered deep in the forests of Madagascar. Scientists had never seen an animal with a furry tail like a fox, big ears like a bat, and large front teeth. What was it? It took over 50 years for scientists to learn that the aye-aye is a kind of **lemur**. Lemurs are a kind of **primate**.

A ring-tailed lemur

AT FIRST, SCIENTISTS THOUGHT THE AYE-AYE WAS A KIND OF SQUIRREL.

Creatures of the Night

When the moon is out, the aye-aye is on the move. It sleeps during the day and travels around its forest home at night. Large, golden-colored eyes and huge, pointy ears help the aye-aye find its way in the dark. Dark, shaggy fur covers an aye-aye's body and bushy tail. It keeps the aye-aye hidden as it moves around the forest.

AYE-AYES ALSO HAVE SOME WHITE FUR. WHEN AN AYE-AYE IS EXCITED OR UPSET, THIS FUR STANDS UP TO MAKE THE ANIMAL LOOK TWICE ITS NORMAL SIZE!

Hanging Out

The aye-aye has large hands and feet with long fingers and toes. All but its big toes end in curved claws. The big toes have a special job. The aye-aye can hang from branches by gripping them with these clawless toes!

The middle finger on each hand is much thinner than the other fingers. It turns out a super thin finger is a helpful tool!

An aye-aye's middle finger

THE AYE-AYE USES
ITS HANDS, FEET, AND
CLAWS TO GROOM
ITS FUR EVERY NIGHT.

Getting Some Grubs

SHH! An aye-aye is trying to find a snack. It munches on wormy **grubs** that tunnel into trees. To find them, the aye-aye *tap-tap-taps* along a branch with its middle finger.

The aye-aye listens until it hears grubs moving under the tree bark. Then, it rips bark off the branch with its teeth. The aye-aye plucks out the grubs with its skinny middle finger and eats them!

AN AYE-AYE HAS CLEAR INNER EYELIDS THAT HELP PROTECT ITS EYES FROM FLYING PIECES OF BARK AS IT GNAWS BRANCHES.

Grubs

A Forest Feast

Along with grubs, the aye-aye eats seeds, **fungus**, and nuts. It also uses its long middle finger to scoop the flesh out of coconuts and mangoes. When eating, the aye-aye is lightning fast. It moves its finger from the food to its mouth about three times per second! The aye-aye uses this finger to drink in the same way. *SLURP!* That's one fancy finger!

THE AYE-AYE WEARS DOWN
ITS FRONT TEETH AS IT EATS.
BUT ITS TEETH KEEP GROWING!

Aye-Ayes in Danger

Aye-ayes are so rarely seen people once thought they were **extinct**. We now know aye-ayes are still around, but the animals are **endangered**. Their forest **habitats** are being cut down. Humans are killing aye-ayes, too. Farmers want to stop aye-ayes from eating their crops. Others fear aye-ayes because some people think they are bad luck.

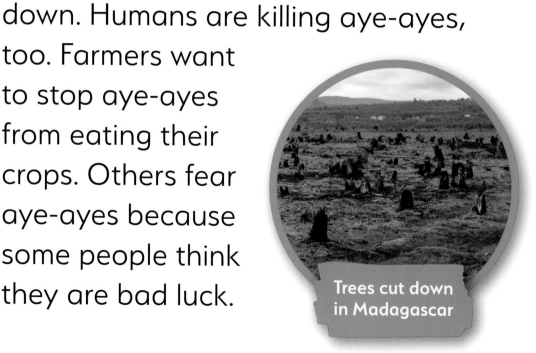

Trees cut down in Madagascar

SOME GROUPS ARE STUDYING AND PROTECTING AYE-AYES. THEY ARE RAISING AYE-AYES IN ZOOS AND ON PROTECTED LANDS.

Safe and Sound

The aye-aye keeps itself safe by staying out of sight. During the day, it curls up in a nest of twigs and leaves. The aye-aye builds several ball-shaped homes high in the forks of tree trunks. At night, the aye-aye spends most of its time moving through the trees between its nests. The aye-aye lives alone.

AYE-AYES ARE MADE FOR LIFE IN THE TREES, NOT ON THE FOREST FLOOR. WHEN THEY HAVE TO WALK ON THE GROUND, THEY RAISE THEIR FINGERS TO PROTECT THEM FROM DAMAGE.

Bringing Up Aye-Ayes

Aye-ayes come together only to **mate**. *Eep! Eep!* A female aye-aye calls out to a male to tell him she is ready. She gives birth to one baby about six months later. The baby drinks milk from its mother's body.

When it is about two years old, the young aye-aye leaves its mother. Soon, it will have babies of its own.

AYE-AYES ARE BORN WITH GREEN EYES.

AYE-AYES ARE AWESOME!
LET'S LEARN EVEN MORE ABOUT THEM.

Kind of animal: Aye-ayes are lemurs. A lemur usually has large eyes, soft fur, and a long tail.

More lemurs: There are over 100 kinds of lemurs. They are found mostly in Madagascar.

Size: Aye-ayes are about 15 inches (38.1 cm) long, not including their tails. That is about the height of a bowling pin.

AYE-AYES AROUND THE WORLD

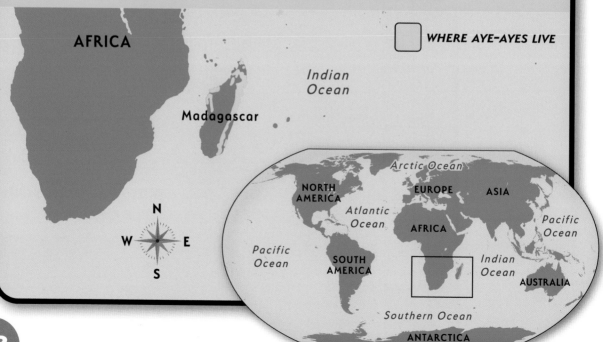

AFRICA

☐ **WHERE AYE-AYES LIVE**

Indian Ocean

Madagascar

N
W   E
S

Arctic Ocean

NORTH AMERICA

EUROPE   ASIA

Atlantic Ocean

AFRICA

Pacific Ocean

Pacific Ocean

SOUTH AMERICA

Indian Ocean

AUSTRALIA

Southern Ocean

ANTARCTICA

endangered in danger of dying out

extinct when a kind of animal has died out completely

fungus a simple living thing that is not a plant or animal; mushrooms are one kind of fungus

grubs the young form of beetles that look like worms

habitats places in nature where animals live

lemur a furry animal that usually has a long tail and large eyes; lemurs are in the primate family and live mainly in Madagascar

mate to come together to have young

primate an animal in the family that includes humans, monkeys, apes, and lemurs

Index

Read More

Arnold, Quinn M. *Aye-Ayes (Creatures of the Night)*. Mankato, MN: Creative Education (2019).

Bassier, Emma. *Aye-Ayes (Weird and Wonderful Animals)*. Minneapolis: Pop! (2020).

Learn More Online

1. **Go to www.factsurfer.com**
2. Enter "**Aye-Aye**" into the search box.
3. Click on the cover of this book to see a list of websites.

About the Author

Colleen Sexton is a writer and editor. She is the author of more than 100 nonfiction books for kids on topics ranging from astronauts to glaciers to sharks. She lives in Minnesota.